ABBA®

GOLD

GREATEST HITS

FLUTE PLAY-ALONG

To acces audio visit:
www.halleonardmgb.com/mylibrary

7179-9785-9360-4250

HAL•LEONARD®

Published by
Hal Leonard

Exclusive Distributors:
Hal Leonard
7777 West Bluemound Road, Milwaukee, WI 53213
Email: info@halleonard.com

Hal Leonard Europe Limited
42 Wigmore Street, Marylebone, London WIU 2 RY
Email: info@halleonardeurope.com

Hal Leonard Australia Pty. Ltd.
4 Lentara Court, Cheltenham, Victoria 9132, Australia
Email: info@halleonard.com.au

Order No. AM996105R
ISBN: 978-1-78558-047-5
This book © Copyright 2015 Hal Leonard

Printed in the EU.

www.halleonard.com

Flute Fingering Chart

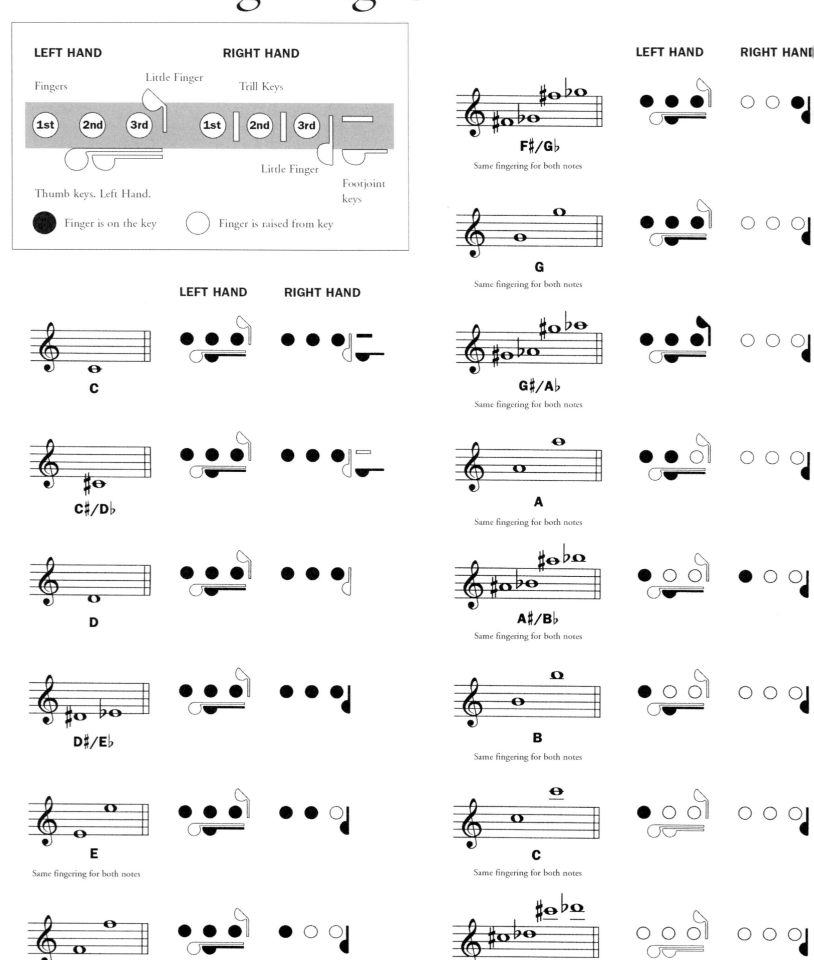

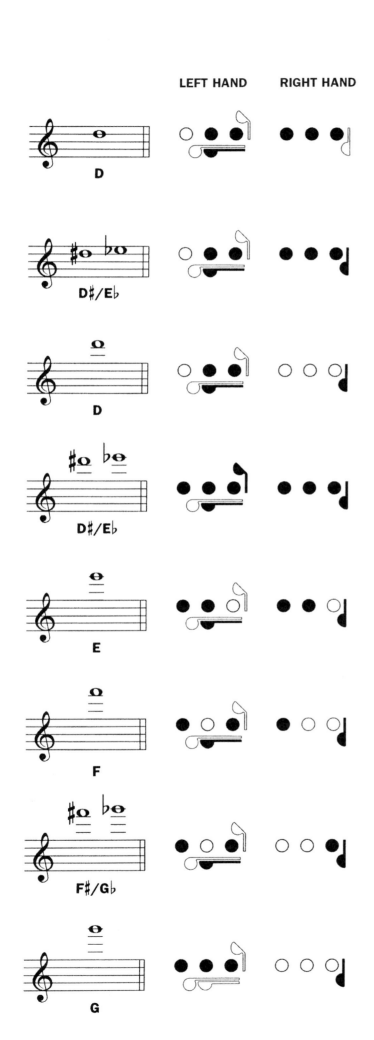

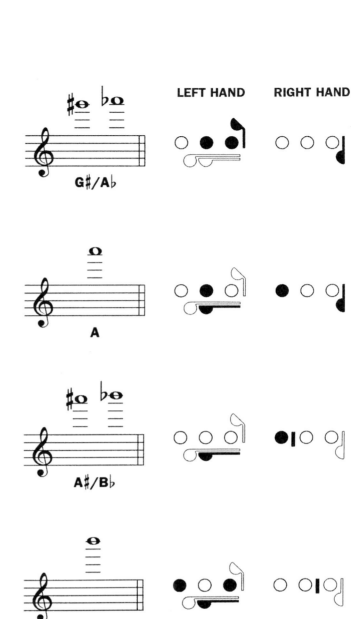

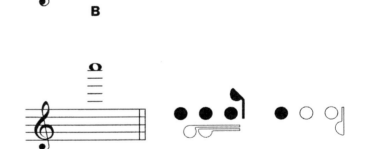

Dancing Queen

Words & Music by Benny Andersson,
Stig Anderson & Björn Ulvaeus

8

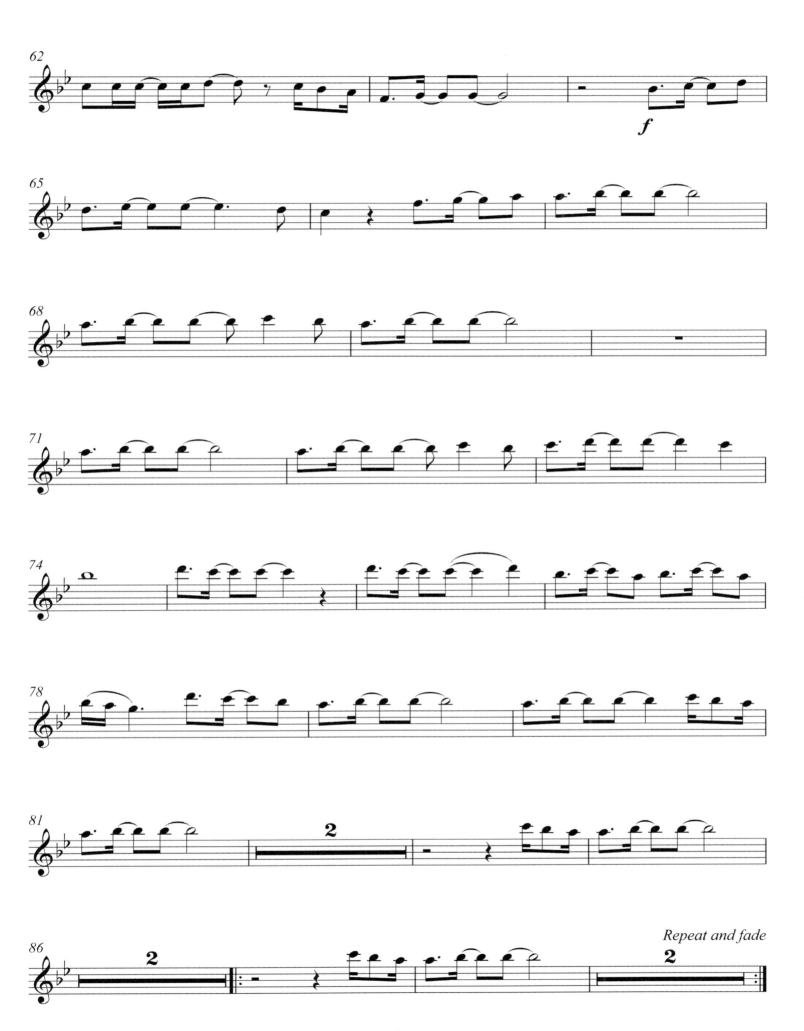

Repeat and fade

9

Knowing Me, Knowing You

Words & Music by Benny Andersson,
Stig Anderson & Björn Ulvaeus

11

Take A Chance On Me

Words & Music by Benny Andersson & Björn Ulvaeus

Mamma Mia

Words & Music by Benny Andersson,
Stig Anderson & Björn Ulvaeus

Repeat and fade

17

Lay All Your Love On Me

Words & Music by Benny Andersson & Björn Ulvaeus

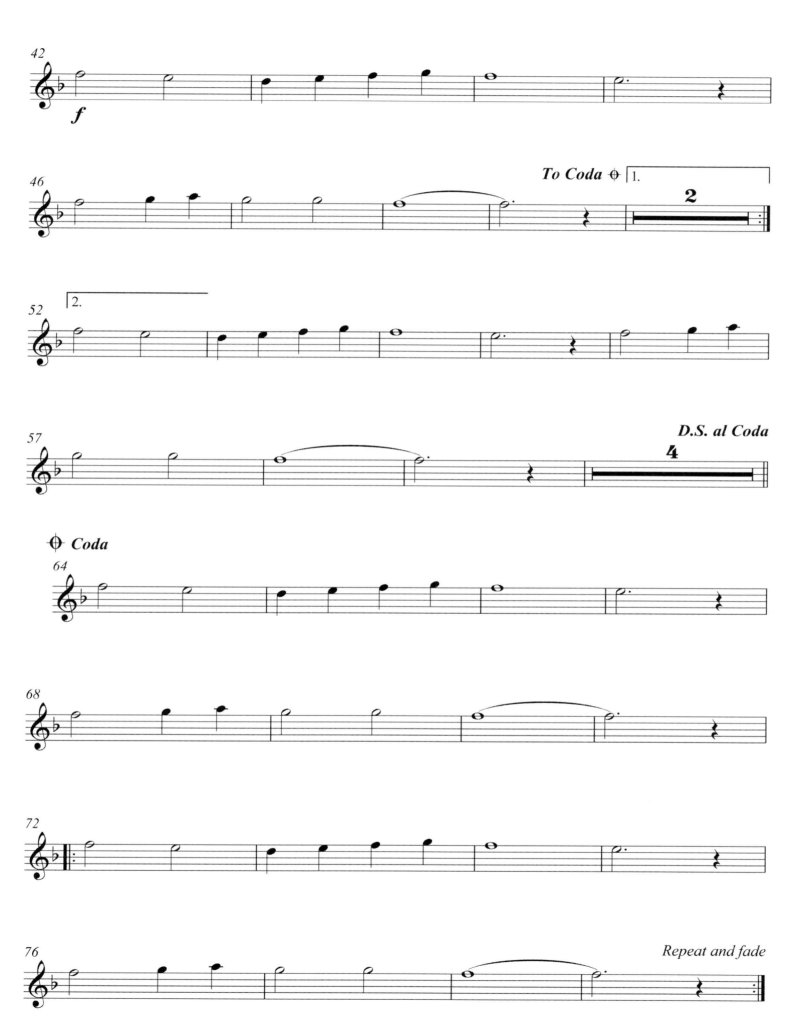

Super Trouper

Words & Music by Benny Andersson & Björn Ulvaeus

I Have A Dream

Words & Music by Benny Andersson & Björn Ulvaeus

The Winner Takes It All

Words & Music by Benny Andersson & Björn Ulvaeus

Money, Money, Money

Words & Music by Benny Andersson & Björn Ulvaeus

S.O.S.

Words & Music by Benny Andersson,
Stig Anderson & Björn Ulvaeus

Moderately

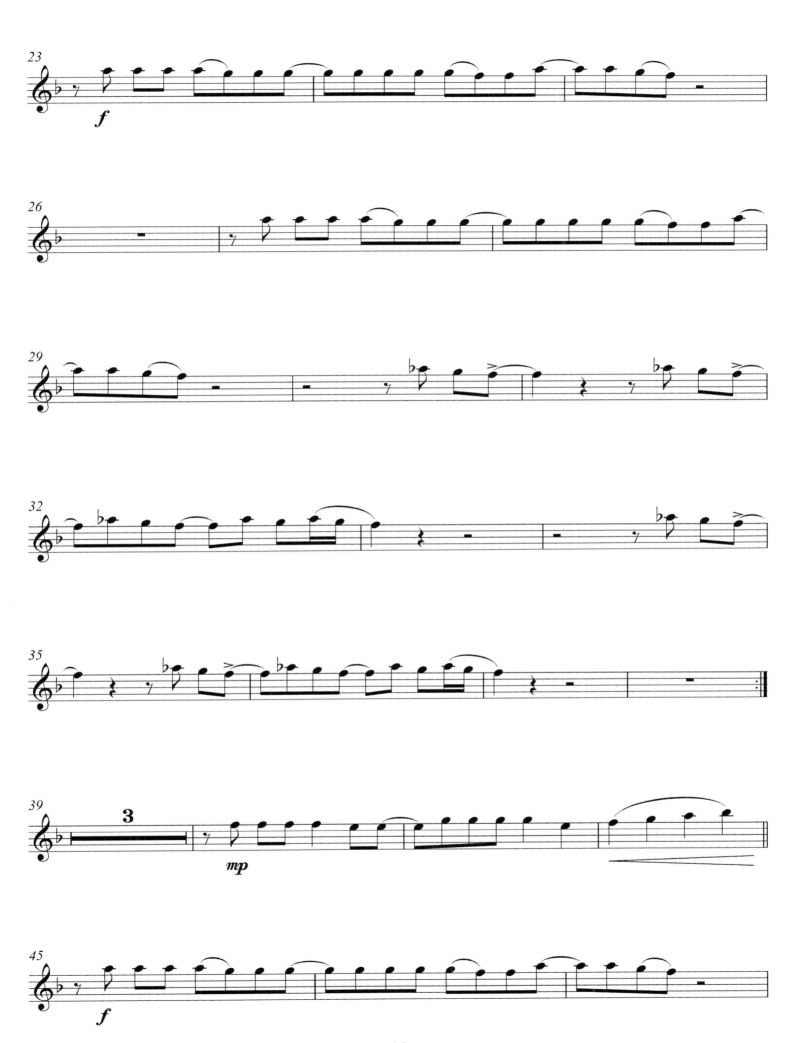

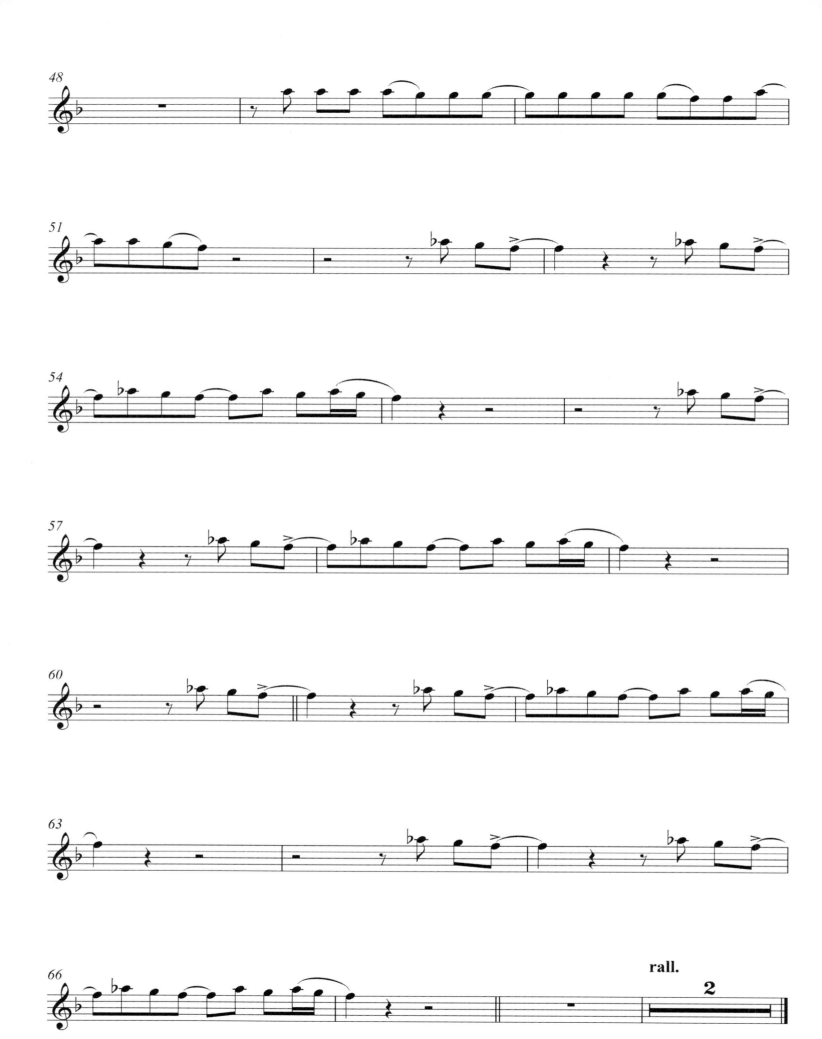

Chiquitita

Words & Music by Benny Andersson & Björn Ulvaeus

Tenderly and lightly

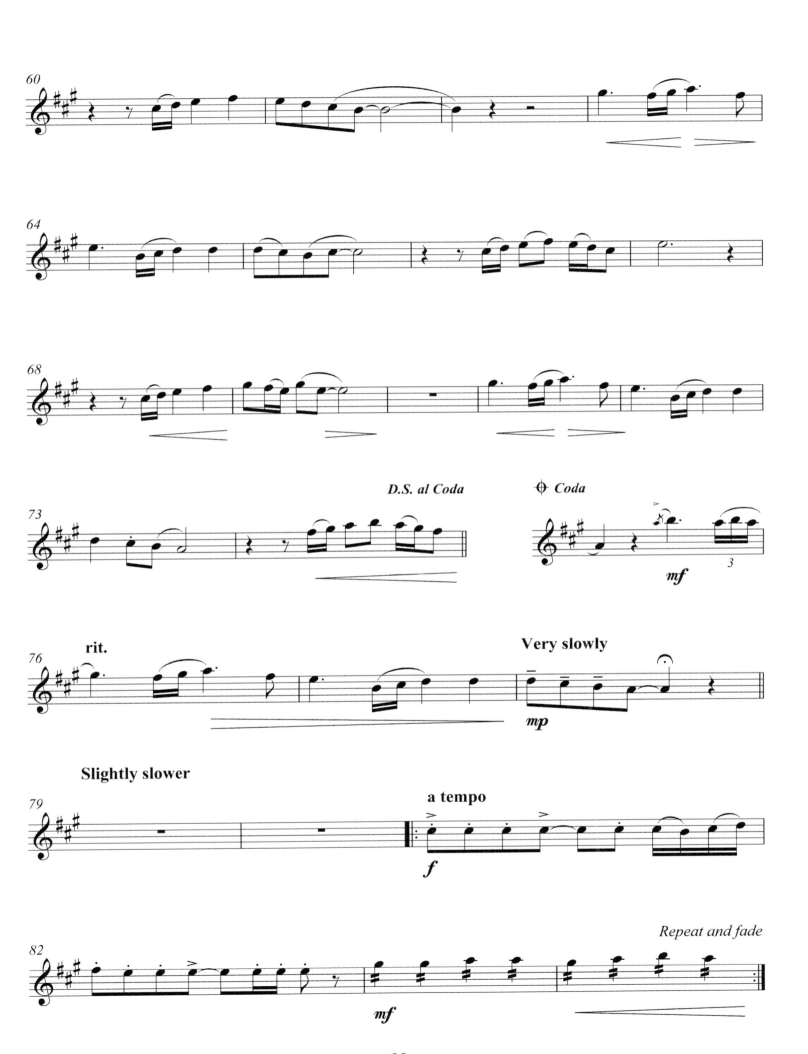

Fernando

Words & Music by Benny Andersson,
Stig Anderson & Björn Ulvaeus

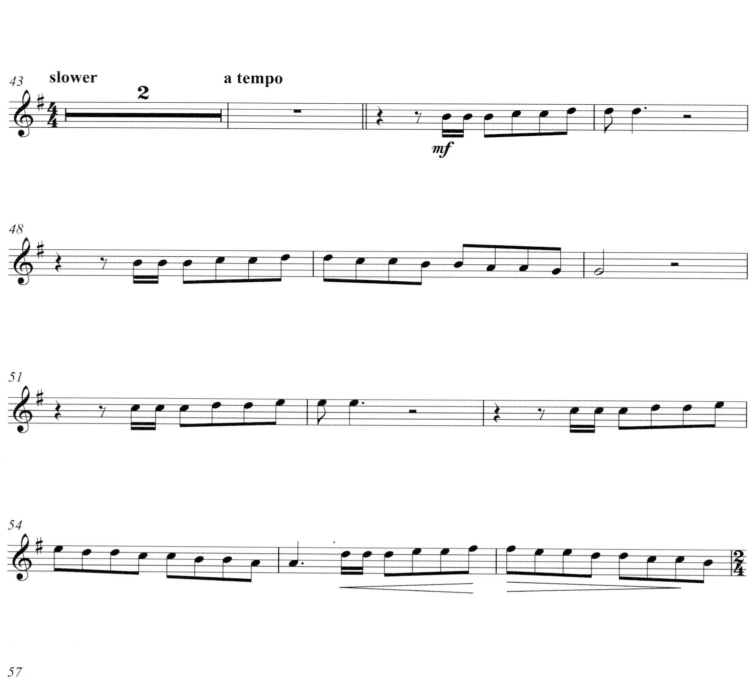

Voulez-Vous

Words & Music by Benny Andersson & Björn Ulvaeus

Bright disco feel

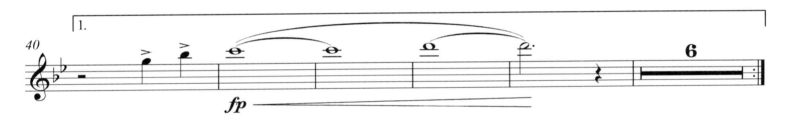

Repeat and fade

40

Gimme! Gimme! Gimme!
(A Man After Midnight)

Words & Music by Benny Andersson & Björn Ulvaeus

Repeat and fade

Does Your Mother Know

Words & Music by Benny Andersson & Björn Ulvaeus

Repeat and fade

One Of Us

Words & Music by Benny Andersson & Björn Ulvaeus

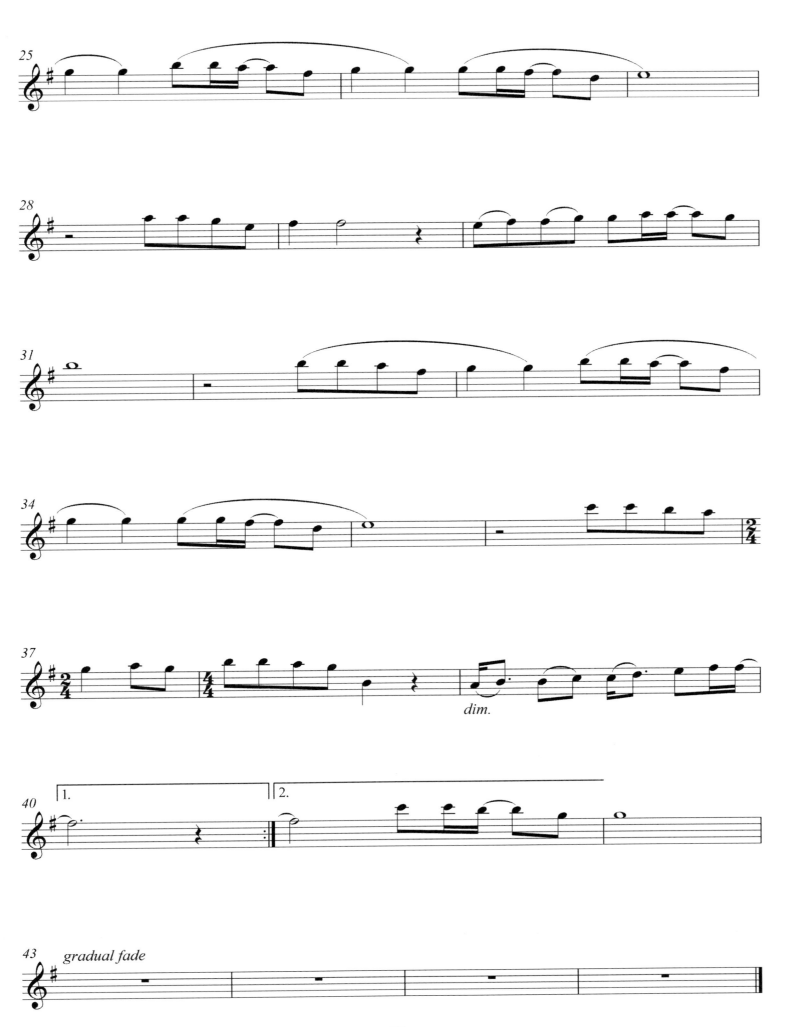

The Name Of The Game

Words & Music by Benny Andersson,
Stig Anderson & Björn Ulvaeus

Repeat and fade

Thank You For The Music

Words & Music by Benny Andersson & Björn Ulvaeus

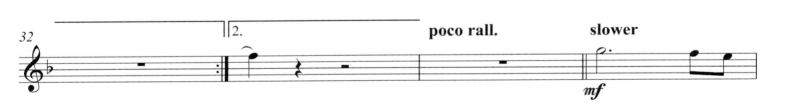

Waterloo

Words & Music by Benny Andersson,
Stig Anderson & Björn Ulvaeus